THE CHUMASH

NATIVE AMERICAN NATIONS

BY BETTY MARCKS
CONSULTANT: TIM TOPPER, CHEYENNE RIVER SIOUX

BLASTOFF! DISCOVERY

BELLWETHER MEDIA • MINNEAPOLIS, MN

Author's Statement of Positionality:
I am a white woman of European descent. As such, I can claim no direct lived experience of being a Native American. In writing this book, however, I have tried to be an ally by relying on sources by Native American writers and authors whenever possible and have worked to let their voices guide its content.

This edition first published in 2025 by Bellwether Media, Inc.

No part of this publication may be reproduced in whole or in part without written permission of the publisher. For information regarding permission, write to Bellwether Media, Inc.,
Attention: Permissions Department,
6012 Blue Circle Drive, Minnetonka, MN 55343.

Library of Congress Cataloging-in-Publication Data

Names: Marcks, Betty, author.
Title: The Chumash / by Betty Marcks.
Description: Minneapolis : Bellwether Media, Inc., 2025. | Series: Blastoff! Discovery: Native American nations | Includes bibliographical references and index.
 | Audience: Ages 7-13 | Audience: Grades 4-6 | Summary: "Engaging images accompany information about the Chumash people. The combination of high-interest subject matter and narrative text is intended for students in grades 3 through 8"
 – Provided by publisher.
Identifiers: LCCN 2024016007 (print) | LCCN 2024016008 (ebook) | ISBN 9798893040067 (library binding) | ISBN 9798893041484 (paperback) | ISBN 9781644879382 (ebook)
Subjects: LCSH: Chumash Indians–Juvenile literature.
Classification: LCC E99.C815 M37 2025 (print) | LCC E99.C815 (ebook) | DDC 979.4004/9758–dc23/eng/20240513
LC record available at https://lccn.loc.gov/2024016007
LC ebook record available at https://lccn.loc.gov/2024016008

Text copyright © 2025 by Bellwether Media, Inc. BLASTOFF! DISCOVERY and associated logos are trademarks and/or registered trademarks of Bellwether Media, Inc. Bellwether Media is a division of Chrysalis Education Group.

Editor: Elizabeth Neuenfeldt   Series Designer: Andrea Schneider
Book Designer: Laura Sowers

Printed in the United States of America, North Mankato, MN.

TABLE OF CONTENTS

THE FIRST PEOPLE	4
TRADITIONAL CHUMASH LIFE	6
EUROPEAN CONTACT	12
LIFE TODAY	16
CONTINUING TRADITIONS	20
FIGHT TODAY, BRIGHT TOMORROW	24
TIMELINE	28
GLOSSARY	30
TO LEARN MORE	31
INDEX	32

THE FIRST PEOPLE

The Chumash are Native American peoples. They call themselves "the first people." The name "Chumash" refers to people from many groups. They all once spoke one of six related languages.

Ancestral Chumash depended on the land and the Pacific Ocean. People lived on four of the Channel Islands in today's California. People also lived in towns across central and southern California. Their homeland stretched along the coast from Paso Robles to Malibu. It spanned inland toward the San Joaquin Valley.

TRADITIONAL CHUMASH LIFE

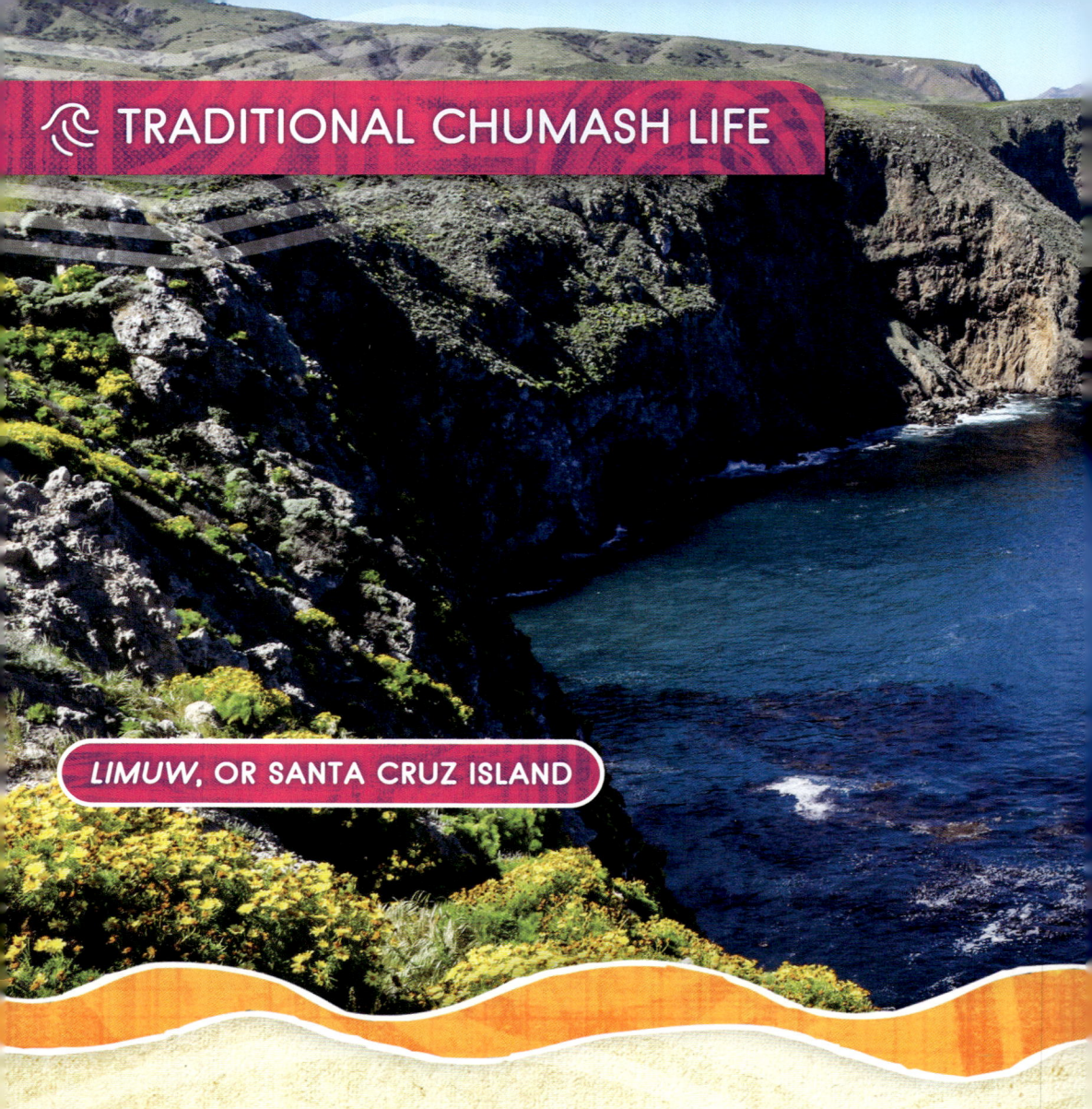

LIMUW, OR SANTA CRUZ ISLAND

Ancestral Chumash lived on the Northern Channel Islands around 13,000 years ago. In their creation story, *Hutash*, the Earth Mother, created the people from seeds on the island *Limuw*. The Earth Mother's husband gave the people fire. The gift helped the people live well. Their villages grew.

The island became crowded. The Earth Mother made a rainbow bridge to the mainland. She told the people to populate the world. Some people made it safely. But those who looked down into the fog fell. She turned them into dolphins. The people call dolphins their brothers and sisters.

The Chumash have used **sacred** sites for thousands of years. Their **traditional** capital is *Tsipxatu*. The site was once used for trade, arts, and more. Another site is *Humqaq*. It is where the souls of those who have passed away start their journey to the next world.

Ancestral Chumash priests made detailed cave paintings. The paintings likely represent important religious figures, natural wonders, and more. The paintings are mostly red, black, and white.

TSIPXATU, OR AVILA BEACH

CAVE PAINTINGS AT CHUMASH PAINTED CAVE STATE HISTORIC PARK

TOMOL

Ancestral Chumash were hunters and gatherers. They used many resources from the land and ocean. They hunted bears, deer, and rabbits on land. They also gathered acorns, seeds, roots, and nuts. Fish, seals, otters, and shellfish were **staples** from the ocean.

Canoes called *tomols* allowed the people to become skilled fishermen and traders. These canoes were most often made from planks of redwood. This wood was lightweight. It did not rot. A mixture of pine tar and other ingredients made the canoes waterproof.

VALUED GOODS

Ancestral Chumash traded goods among themselves. They also traded with other Native American nations. Shells, beadwork, baskets, and carvings were popular goods.

CHUMASH RESOURCES

REDWOOD

PINE RESIN

WOOD ASH

PINE TAR

HEMP

TOMOL

EUROPEAN CONTACT

DISPLAY OF TRADITIONAL CHUMASH HOUSES AT THE CHUMASH INDIAN MUSEUM

Ancestral Chumash had well-established villages. They had a complex social system. It was made up of different **hierarchies**. But life began to change when they met Europeans in 1542. Europeans brought diseases that the Chumash had never had before. Many Chumash lost their lives to these diseases. Conflicts occurred as well.

The Spanish began creating **missions** on the mainland starting in 1772. Soon, Chumash life changed forever. The Spanish forced them to build the missions. They also destroyed the Chumash social system. Thousands of Chumash lost their lives.

CEMETERY AT THE SANTA BARBARA MISSION

Some Chumash moved to missions to survive. This caused many villages to break apart. The Chumash were treated cruelly in the missions. The Spanish took their freedoms. The hardships the Chumash endured led to the Chumash **Revolt** of 1824. They took over the missions. But the Spanish soon took them back.

ARTWORK OF THE CHUMASH REVOLT OF 1824

FAMOUS CHUMASH

KARISSA VALENCIA

BIRTHDAY August 1991

FAMOUS FOR
The creator of the Netflix series *Spirit Rangers* that celebrates Chumash and Cowlitz cultures

CHUMASH WOMEN AND CHILD OUTSIDE A MISSION

The missions ended in the 1830s. But the Chumash continued to experience the hardships of **colonization**. Europeans forced them to give up much of their land. Many Chumash lost their lives. But those who survived did not give up. They fought to keep their **culture** alive.

LIFE TODAY

Today, there are nearly 5,000 members of the Chumash nation. More than 250 members live on the Santa Ynez **Band** of Chumash Indians **reservation**. It is in Southern California. The reservation spans more than 2.3 square miles (6.1 square kilometers). This includes some of the nation's original tribal lands. Members also live in other parts of Southern California.

Many other people are members of other Chumash bands. Some people are members of the Tejon Indian Tribe. Their reservation is in Bakersfield, California.

The government of the Santa Ynez Band is led by the nation's Business Committee. These elected officials make legal and business decisions. The Tribal Elders **Council** maintains the people's history, **heritage**, and traditions. Tribal **Administration** oversees programs that help members.

GOVERNMENT OF THE SANTA YNEZ BAND OF CHUMASH INDIANS

BUSINESS COMMITTEE
- Chairman
- Vice Chairman
- Secretary-Treasurer
- two additional members

TRIBAL ELDERS COUNCIL

TRIBAL ADMINISTRATION

GAMING COMMISSION

CHUMASH CASINO RESORT

The government also manages the Chumash Casino Resort. Members of the Gaming **Commission** make sure the casino follows state and federal rules. The Chumash Casino Resort is an important part of the band's economy. Money made from the casino goes to different programs for members. They include health care and education.

CONTINUING TRADITIONS

PETRA PICO, FAMOUS CHUMASH BASKET WEAVER

Many people practice the traditions of their Chumash ancestors. Chumash baskets have been praised for their quality and beauty for thousands of years. Weavers make traditional baskets to connect to the land and plants. The practice also helps bring awareness to the health of **native** plants.

The baskets are often made with juncus plants. The green stems become tan when they dry. The roots are red. Weavers may dye the stems black. These colors allow weavers to add designs. Weavers may use nontraditional materials as well. These can include horsehair or waxed thread.

A WATERTIGHT WEAVE

Chumash baskets can be woven very tightly. Some can hold water!

TRADITIONAL CHUMASH BASKETS

Ancestral Chumash used baskets for many things. Some were used as hats. Sometimes baskets stored special items. They also helped people gather food and cook.

JUNCUS

BLACK WALNUT

CHUMASH BASKET

The Santa Ynez Band has taken major steps to bring back their Samala language. The government created a language program in 2008. A dictionary was also developed to help people learn the language.

STREET SIGN IN SAMALA AT VANDENBERG SPACE FORCE BASE MEANING "OUR GATHERING PLACE FOR JUNCUS"

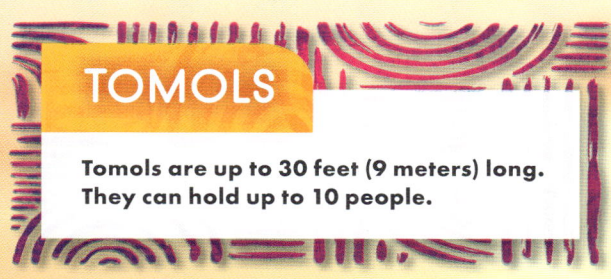

TOMOLS

Tomols are up to 30 feet (9 meters) long. They can hold up to 10 people.

Many people engage in other traditions. One is the annual historic tomol crossing. A crew crosses the Santa Barbara Channel to Santa Cruz Island in a tomol. The trip can take around eight hours! On the island, people celebrate Chumash culture on their sacred ancestral land.

FIGHT TODAY, BRIGHT TOMORROW

PART OF THE PROPOSED CHUMASH HERITAGE NATIONAL MARINE SANCTUARY

Many Native American nations are fighting for their lands. The Chumash are working to gain control of 7,000 square miles (18,130 square kilometers) of the Pacific Ocean. It would become the Chumash Heritage National Marine **Sanctuary**. They have proposed becoming co-managers of the waters. Approval of the sanctuary would protect the waters from business development.

SUPPORTERS AT A RALLY FOR THE MARINE SANCTUARY

A wind energy project may also be approved. Some people feel this project would help fight **climate change**. But not everyone agrees with the project. It would mean developing on a sacred site. It would also make the sanctuary smaller.

The Santa Ynez Chumash Environmental Office (SYCEO) believes climate change will harm historical lands. It expects more days of extreme heat each year. There will likely be changes in rain patterns. There could be more wildfires, too. These effects will impact the daily lives and cultural practices of Chumash people.

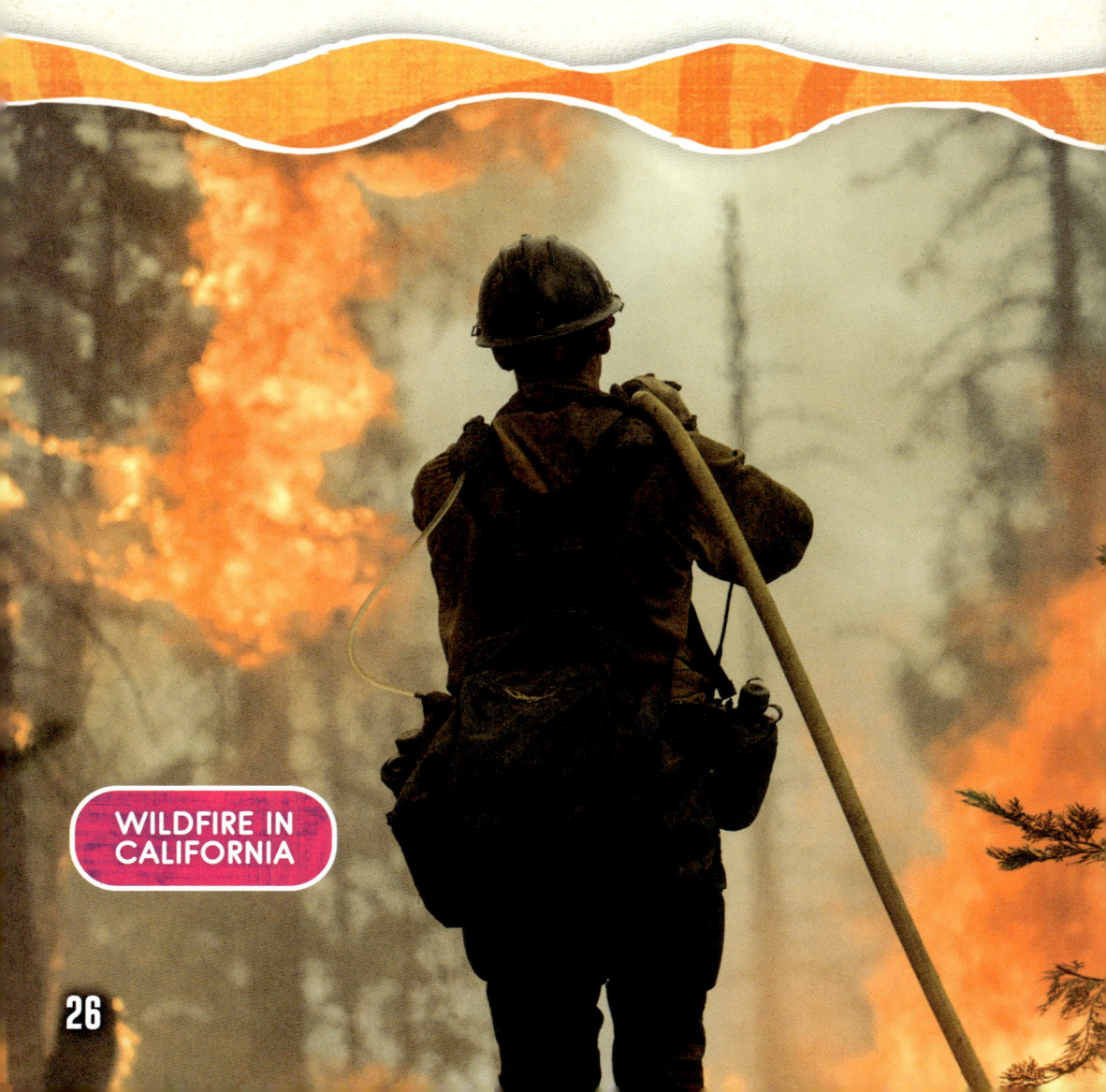

WILDFIRE IN CALIFORNIA

SANTA YNEZ VALLEY

Members of SYCEO work to combat climate change. They grow native plants to restore the land. They provide solutions to areas where **pollution** is a problem. Their efforts help the earth. Their work strengthens their culture!

TIMELINE

1542
Ancestral Chumash encounter Europeans for the first time

EARLY 1800s
The last of the island Chumash move to the mainland

1901
The Santa Ynez Band of Chumash Indians becomes federally recognized by the U.S.

1772
The first Spanish missions are established in mainland Chumash villages

1824
Chumash successfully take over a number of missions for a short period of time during the Chumash Revolt of 1824

1976
The first tomol is built and launched in over 140 years

Violet Sage Walker and other Chumash members fight to create and become co-managers of the Chumash Heritage National Marine Sanctuary

2023

1914
John P. Harrington begins working with María Solares to record the Samala language

2008
The Santa Ynez Band creates a Samala language program

1980
Channel Islands National Park and Channel Islands National Marine Sanctuary are established

GLOSSARY

administration—a group of people who oversee parts of a government

ancestral—related to relatives who lived long ago

band—a group of people who live as a community and share a culture

climate change—a human-caused change in Earth's weather due to warming temperatures

colonization—the act of taking over another nation for power

commission—a group of people who carry out a job

council—a group of people who meet to run a government

culture—the beliefs, arts, and ways of life in a place or society

heritage—the traditions, achievements, and beliefs that are part of the history of a group of people

hierarchies—groups of persons or things arranged in ranks or classes

missions—settlements made to spread a religion

native—originally from the area or having begun in the area

pollution—substances that make an area dirty and not safe for use

reservation—land set aside by the U.S. government for the forced removal of a Native American community from their original land

revolt—an often violent uprising against a leader

sacred—relating to spiritual or religious practice

sanctuary—a place that provides protection or shelter

staples—widely used foods or other items

traditional—related to customs, ideas, or beliefs handed down from one generation to the next

TO LEARN MORE

AT THE LIBRARY

Oachs, Emily Rose. *California*. Minneapolis, Minn.: Bellwether Media, 2022.

Santa Ynez Band of Chumash Indians, Richard B. Applegate, et al. *Samala-English Dictionary*. Santa Ynez, Calif.: Santa Ynez Band of Chumash Indians, 2007.

Sorrel, Traci. *We Are Still Here!: Native American Truths Everyone Should Know*. Watertown, Mass.: Charlesbridge, 2021.

ON THE WEB

FACTSURFER

Factsurfer.com gives you a safe, fun way to find more information.

1. Go to www.factsurfer.com.
2. Enter "the Chumash" into the search box and click 🔍.
3. Select your book cover to see a list of related content.

INDEX

bands, 16
Channel Islands, 4, 6, 7, 23
Chumash Casino Resort, 19
Chumash Heritage National Marine Sanctuary, 24, 25
Chumash resources, 10, 11
Chumash Revolt of 1824, 14
climate change, 25, 26, 27
colonization, 15
council, 18
culture, 4, 6, 7, 8, 10, 11, 12, 13, 15, 22, 23, 26, 27
foods, 10
future, 24, 25, 26, 27
government of the Santa Ynez Band of Chumash Indians, 18, 19, 22
heritage, 18
history, 4, 6, 7, 10, 11, 12, 13, 14, 15, 17, 18
homeland, 4, 6, 15, 16, 23, 24, 26
languages, 4, 22
Limuw, 6
map, 4, 16
members, 16, 18, 19
missions, 13, 14, 15
name, 4
Pacific Ocean, 4, 10, 24
reservation, 16, 17
Samala, 22
Santa Ynez Band of Chumash Indians, 16, 17, 18, 19, 22
Santa Ynez Chumash Environmental Office, 26, 27
Tejon Indian Tribe, 16
timeline, 28–29
tomols, 10, 11, 23
traditional Chumash baskets, 20, 21
traditions, 8, 10, 11, 12, 18, 20, 21, 23
Valencia, Karissa, 14

The images in this book are reproduced through the courtesy of: Eyal Nahmias/ Alamy, cover, p. 21 (a watertight weave); North Wind Picture Archives/ Alamy, p. 3; Andy Konieczny, pp. 4-5; Bram Reusen, pp. 6-7; Andrea Izzotti, p. 7; Mario Ramirez, p. 8; Carol M. Highsmith/ Wikipedia, pp. 8-9, 13; Robert Schwemmer/ NOAA, p. 10; MET/ BOT/ Alamy, p. 11 (valued goods); Lucky-photographer, p. 11 (redwood); twinlynx, p. 11 (pine resin); Anna Hollan, p. 11 (wood ash); meunierd, p. 11 (hemp); Angel Wynn/ NativeStock, pp. 11 (tomol), 21 (basket); Leigh Green/ Alamy, p. 12; Alexander Harmer/ Wikipedia, p. 14 (artwork of the Chumash Revolt of 1824); Karissa Valencia/ Karissa Valencia, p. 14 (Karissa Valencia); Netflix/ Everett Collection, p. 14 (*Spirit Rangers*); unknown/ Wikipedia, pp. 15, 20 (Petra Pico); Spencer Weiner/ Getty Images, pp. 16-17; VexilloYT/ Wikipedia, pp. 18 (flag), 28 (1901); Bobjgalindo/ Wikipedia, p. 19; Nik Wheeler/ Getty Images, p. 20; Anthony Valois/ Wikipedia, p. 21 (juncus); MacBen, p. 21 (black walnut); Joshua LeRoi/ Wikipedia, p. 22; CINMS, p. 23; Mario Tama/ Getty Images, pp. 24-25, 25, 29 (2023); Kari Greer/ USFS/ Wikipedia, p. 26; Let Go Media, p. 27; Chris06/ Wikipedia, p. 28 (1772); Kelly vanDellen, p. 29 (1980).